Bearing Witness

Quilts and Stories Honoring Life in a Children's Hospital

Julie Hliboki

Transilient Publishing
ISBN # 978-0-9832602-4-0

Transilient Publishing

Every child's story is precious. I dedicate the quilts and this booklet to all of the children whose lives profoundly affected me, as well as their families. I also dedicate this booklet to the hospital staff—chaplains, nurses, doctors, social workers, and countless others—who selflessly commit themselves to the compassionate care of sick children. My greatest hope for the reader is that, by discovering yourself in this work, your own compassionate impulse will be strengthened and you will share your own stories.

Introduction

I am a Quaker interfaith chaplain. For the past several years, my role as a chaplain has focused mainly on providing spiritual care in hospice and hospital settings. In 2015, I spent eight intensive months as a chaplain intern/resident in a pediatric hospital. I ministered to more than 1,000 patients and families as well as hospital staff in several areas throughout the hospital.

It is hard to describe in a succinct way the day-to-day chaplaincy needs in a pediatric hospital. For example, in just one 12-hour charge shift where I was the only chaplain in the entire hospital, I attended to nine traumas and eight other chaplaincy requests. The traumas included three gunshot wounds, three motor vehicle collisions, two children hit by cars, and an impalement. During this difficult day, I ministered to the families of these trauma patients and to those hospital staff who were taxed emotionally and physically. The last trauma of that day involved a child who had been hit by a car and was in critical condition. The child's mother was distraught, angry, and shaking with fear. I provided for the mom a calming, non-anxious presence, empathetic listening, water and food, a steady hand at the child's bedside, a connection to the nursing staff, hugs and physical reassurance, prayer and spiritual support, and attentiveness to other family members as they arrived. Later that evening, the child died and I aided the family in selecting a funeral home, and created a memory box that contained the child's hand- and foot-prints, a lock of hair, and bereavement materials. This was just *one* day at the hospital.

To minister in a hospital setting full of such encounters, I practiced, moment-to-moment, being present to each person I met, allowed myself to be touched deeply, and responded to the emergent need. As a result, I was able to provide rich spiritual care to hundreds of people, but the intensity and weight of what I witnessed and experienced accumulated. After eight months of pediatric chaplaincy, on top of two years of hospice and other chaplaincy services, I needed time to assimilate all that I had faced.

These quilts and stories arose as a way for me to integrate and process, and perhaps release, what I continued to carry with me. The quilts came first. As I thought about a child, I would allow that memory to guide my hand in selecting material and in designing the quilt pattern. As I sewed the quilts, I lifted up prayers of love and compassion for the child, his or her family, the caregivers, and anyone else dealing with a similar issue.

Each quilt tells part of the child's story. I taught myself how to quilt as I went, which means that the all of quilts have one or two imperfections. I like this, and intentionally left the imperfections since they speak to the raw, messy humanness in my life. On the back of each quilt is a small tag that says, "you are loved." As I visited children and families, it was of the utmost importance to me to convey how much they are loved by their caregivers, the Sacred, and me.

After completing each quilt, a story* unfolded. The child's medical condition was often just the tip of the iceberg for what his or her family had to manage. Many families struggled with hardships including inadequate nourishing food for healing, difficulty getting time off work to visit their child, the absence of child care for siblings who were not sick, lack of resources to purchase food from the hospital cafeteria, outside pressure to make end-of-life decisions, stress leading to conflict or violence among family members…the list is very long. As the quilt project progressed, so did my desire that it help reveal to a larger audience the challenges and suffering that so many families face each day, as well as their ability to face these difficulties with courage and dignity.

Each of the hundreds of children, families, and caregivers I ministered to during those eight months touched me deeply. All of them forever changed me. These encounters were precious to me, and exposed the part of me that was willing to open myself over and over to unfathomable intimacy with complete strangers, and they with me. Many incidents brought me to my knees, figuratively and literally, and often to tears. These memories unleash a tenderness and compassion in me that leaves me feeling vulnerable and humbled, yet I have also gained strength and resiliency. I recognize that such stories are universal and can be found in hospitals around the world. My deep desire is that every child's story is cherished.

When I began this project, I thought perhaps that creating the quilts and writing the stories would ease the intensity of the memories and release them from my body. It hasn't worked that way. The relationships with each child, family, and hospital caregiver continue in me. The form of those relationships has shifted, but I imagine they will be with me for the rest of my life. I willingly allowed myself to be opened, and gave all I had to answer each call. Thus, these experiences are etched in my heart.

What *has* happened by creating and sharing this body of work is that I no longer feel alone holding these encounters. All who view these pieces come along side me and bear witness in their own way. Each family who has had a sick child joins the abiding, and every hospital chaplain, nurse, technician, doctor, and pastoral caregiver will have his or her own story to share. Collectively, we can hold these experiences—and more—with greater love and compassion, which I believe will eventually help all who are suffering.

Thank you for bearing witness with me.

Julie

* *To protect privacy, the names and stories were fictionalized and do not refer to any singular child or family. Rather, these composite stories represent the stories of millions of children and families in hospitals around the world.*

Quilts and Stories

Kamal

Kamal is a chunky, eighteen-month-old boy with a ton of energy. The chaplains, nurses, and other hospital staff affectionately call him "Chunky Buddy." His continual grin, sparkling eyes, and mischievous giggle capture the heart of nearly everyone he encounters. When he decided that the large blue button on the wall was too irresistible not to touch, he set off a hospital-wide "code blue" alarm that sent many of us running into his room. Staring at us with big, wide eyes and a huge smile, we couldn't have any other response than to laugh . . . and move his crib away from the wall!

In the eight months I spent visiting Kamal who suffered from a variety of illnesses, I only met Kamal's mom once. In her early twenties, she and her five children lived with Kamal's grandma, and she worked a part-time job. Between working and caring for her children, she had little time to be with Kamal. She expressed this to me matter-of-factly, and I imagined I could see in her weariness that she saw no other way of coping with time away from Kamal. I felt distressed by the complexity of her situation, the challenges of generational poverty, and the circumstances that led to giving to several children at such a young age.

Kamal had many toys in his crib. His favorite was a wind-up mobile decorated with brightly colored plastic flowers. Whenever I entered his room, he would point to the mobile and I would wind it for him. As the mobile played music, we would hold hands while I whispered to Kamal how much he was loved—by me, by his mom, by the nurses, and by God. His beautiful, chubby face beamed joy as he searched my eyes and my soul in pursuit of this truth. After a visit with Kamal, there was usually a spring in my step, spawned by his irresistible delight. He is etched in my heart.

Mwele

I met Mwele the day after she was born. She was very ill and awaiting surgery. Mwele's mom was from Nigeria. The hospital was a scary place for her, especially being alone and so far from home. After Mwele's surgery, I spent time with her and her mom nearly every day, ending each visit by hearing mom's prayers. Together, mom and I watched Mwele grow stronger and gain weight. We were elated when she was finally stable enough for mom to hold and feed her. The nurses made Mwele a colorful name sign and a mobile of African safari animals.

When Mwele was three weeks old, I heard over the hospital intercom system a "code blue" alert indicating that a patient had a cardiac arrest. I listened for the announcement of the floor and room where the code blue was occurring and recognized Mwele's coordinates. I ran up the stairs to her room with a sinking feeling, hoping that the code blue was a false alarm as they sometimes are. This one was real. Mwele had experienced a cardiac arrest. Mom was standing by her bedside shaking, sobbing, and praying. We dropped to our knees together and I held mom while she petitioned God for a miracle. Mwele was resuscitated, but her condition was poor.

Mwele continued to decline. Mom was beside herself with grief. She did not think she could bear her daughter dying, especially after forming such a strong bond through breastfeeding. My heart ached for her. I taught mom breathing techniques, and encouraged her to eat, get rest, and connect with her family in Africa. The nurses who were with Mwele 24-hours a day cared for Mwele lovingly and provided evening respites for mom.

At four weeks old, Mwele's little heart stopped beating and she was placed on a life-support machine. A day later, as we shed tears and said prayers, Mwele's mom gave permission to stop the machine and allowed Mwele to die naturally. Mom's courage and dignity remain with me to this day.

Annabelle

Annabelle is a beautiful, tiny three-month-old infant, with fuzzy blond hair, a crooked smile, and gentle snores. Her peaceful smile and sleepy eyes melt my heart the first time we meet. Alone in her crib without any family present, Annabelle lies quietly, barely aware of the medical devices surrounding her. My heart reaches out to her as I hold her tiny hand, sing to her, and remind Annabelle how much she is loved. I offer this reassurance to Annabelle every day, and encourage her to heal and grow stronger.

After a week or so, I finally meet Annabelle's mom, a young woman who is struggling to learn how to bond with Annabelle. She is reluctant to hold or feed Annabelle or even sit near her, and seems incapable of connecting. When I am present, mom is often trying to reach Annabelle's father, who cannot visit because of previous episodes of domestic violence. I wonder if her identity and self-worth are wrapped up in his approval of her since she fears being without him. I feel compassion for mom and sadness for how this may affect her relationship with Annabelle.

Fortunately, the next week, I meet Annabelle's aunts, one by one. These beautiful women recognized mom's inability to care for Annabelle at this crucial time. They take turns sitting with and loving Annabelle 24-hours a day. Each shares with me that Annabelle is a precious gift for the entire family and that they have all fallen in love with her. They look forward to loving and caring for Annabelle throughout her life. I am relieved and trust that this love extends to mom, too.

I am forever shaped by the determination of these collective women, the love they showered upon Annabelle, and their willingness to step in while Annabelle's mom struggles through her own issues. My prayer is that Annabelle will continue to thrive in the midst of this love.

Unimaginable

On a beautiful, crisp February winter morning my pager alerts me to an incoming airlifted trauma. The text reads 5-year-old, GSW (gunshot wound), stat, critical condition, 10 minutes out. As I head to the Emergency Department (ED), my pager sounds again, this time reading 6-year-old, GSW, 10 minutes out . . . and another minute later, 7-year-old, GSW, 10 minutes out. My presumption is that dispatch is correcting the age of the incoming patient, however when I enter the ED I see the staff scrambling to don blue plastic gowns and sending teams into three trauma rooms. "Dear Lord," I think, "what happened?"

The charge nurse informs me that there has been a mass shooting of children. I am stunned. Some of the children are being flown to our hospital. I try to take in the unimaginable. I begin to silently pray, "Lord have mercy" as I check on the staff in each trauma room to see if they need anything before the children arrive. I find them in stellar, professional, warrior mode as the patients enter on stretchers.

The nurses, doctors, and technicians are remarkable in their mastery, attentiveness, and tenderness for the patients. One child dies, and several nurses pray with me while we surround this little one and hold him in the Light. The other children are stabilized and whisked off to surgery. As I converse with the remaining staff about what we witnessed, we learn that the shooter is now dead, too. We stand together in shocked grief, speechless in the face of such violence, aching over the immense suffering. In our deep vulnerability, there are no words, only the silent presence of our connection to each other and the Holy.

Tabatha

On a pre-dawn winter morning, I enter the hospital chapel to center myself, meditate, and lift up prayers before starting rounds for the day. In the gentle glow of the chapel's low lighting, I see an older woman sitting in a chair quietly weeping with her hands clasped over her heart. I sit next to her in the otherwise empty room, silently breathing a Tonglen practice—inhaling her pain and suffering, exhaling relief and peace. She takes my hand and together we sit as the sunlight begins to fill the room.

Her name is Rachel. I learn that she and her husband have adopted several special-needs children of various ages. They felt a calling to adopt after their own child was grown and off to college. Nine months ago, they adopted another child who had been abandoned by her meth-addicted birth mother. Tabatha, or Tabby, was admitted to the hospital once again last night and Rachel is exhausted. Still, her face brightens as she tells me about Tabby and invites me to meet her. We leave the chapel and head upstairs to Tabby's hospital room.

Tabby is a miracle baby like so many children who live through seemingly impossible illnesses. She was not expected to survive more than a few days, and here she is almost two years old, grinning from ear to ear. Tabby is as cute as can be. Visually, only her constant and unsynchronized eye movements, like marbles rolling every which way, reveal her challenges. Mom hands Tabby to me to hold and I drink in her preciousness. She tells me that Tabby swims between this world and the next, and she is thankful to have been given such a gift. Mom is grateful for every day she has with Tabby.

I am in awe of this woman—her commitment and strength and love in the midst of her deep, penetrating exhaustion. I ask her what moved her to adopt these children, how she finds strength to keep going, and where she learned such love and compassion. She responds with one word—faith. We sit in silence together, letting "faith" sink into our bones. As I pass Tabby back to her, I know that my life has been transformed.

Jackson

My pager alerts me to an incoming victim of trauma, a fourteen-year-old male, gunshot wound. In anticipation, my mind scans the possibilities—gang violence, carelessness and accidental shooting, or attempted suicide. As I enter the Emergency Department (ED), the Charge Nurse confirms it is the latter. My heart sinks. It is the third gunshot wound of the day brought to our pediatric hospital, and it is only 2:00 pm. What is going on out there?

The airlift helicopter gurney arrives in the trauma room. Jackson's face and skull are covered in blood. The doctors, nurses, and technicians, wearing blue plastic full-body aprons rush to his care as the paramedics shout out his vital statistics. For a few seconds I survey the scene, an incredibly well rehearsed orchestra led by a seasoned conductor. The doctor in charge gives prompts, but the twenty or so members of the trauma room medical team already know what to do. I realize that they have probably responded to similar crises hundreds of times. I say a silent prayer and leave the room to find Jackson's mom and dad.

In another room, they sit with a social worker. Jackson's mom is sobbing, pounding on his father's chest, pleading that his guns be removed from the house. They have five other children, all younger than Jackson. His dad is adamant that he has a right to keep guns in his home, that this gun was locked up, and that he has no idea how Jackson accessed the gun. I am stunned by the father's proclamation of his right to bear arms at this moment, but also realize that it arises from his shock, fear, and grief, unable to accept his son's condition in the room next door. The social worker asks what happened. We learn that after being reprimanded for a minor infraction, Jackson went outside and shot himself.

I'm called back into the trauma room. Jackson has died. I devote the next hour or so to him, the medical team, and his parents, offering spiritual sustenance and strength. Jackson's mom and dad are holding each other closely in deep sorrow. Afterwards, I head outdoors for my own sacred restoration. I give thanks for the life that is blooming all around me—for the palate of floral colors and for the children playing tag—and pray for greater wisdom for our politicians whose choices so deeply affect the growing tragedy of gun violence.

Charlie

Charlie is five days old, a plump baby boy who mostly sleeps. This morning at 6:30 am, Charlie and his family are in the pre-op Day Surgery unit. Dressed in blue and yellow jammies, he is peacefully sleeping in his mother's arms. Charlie's dad and big brother (four years old) are watching TV. I sense it is a distraction to help them cope with the uncertainty this day will bring. Charlie was born with an illness that compromises his heart. In an hour or so, Charlie will receive the first of a series of complicated surgical procedures to address his condition.

The family asks for prayer before the surgery. We petition God to guide the hands of the surgeon and nurses, to heal Charlie's heart, and to give them the courage and strength to manage this unexpected crisis. I learn that Charlie's family lives four hours away, that dad will lose his hourly-paid construction job if he misses work, and that mom has no one in this area to call on for support. They wear the weariness of these added stresses visibly on their faces. Even big brother is exhausted from the early morning drive.

Unfortunately, Charlie continued to decline. Since his family was only able to visit on Sundays, his nurses stepped in to give Charlie essential love and support. Each day when I visited Charlie with prayer and spiritual presence, I would find his nurse by his bedside tending to him lovingly. The dedication, energy, and skill of these nurses touched me deeply. I had observed their sophisticated medical expertise, but now I also witnessed their tenderness and affection for Charlie.

At 22 days, Charlie drew his last breath. The nurses and I circle around his tiny medical bed holding hands, shedding tears, and loving him into his next journey. I am grateful for the presence of such love in his short life.

Jaymar

On a frosty winter windy Sunday, fallen brown oak leaves blow in bunches, forming funnels and eddies. The sun shines brightly but it is cold outside. I am grateful for the warmth and quiet of the hospital chapel. As I sit in silent meditation, my pager alerts me to an incoming trauma via helicopter—an eleven-year-old male in critical condition.

It appears that Jaymar has hung himself. When the paramedics arrived, they found Jaymar on the brink of death and resuscitated him. They are yelling these details to us as Jaymar is wheeled into the trauma room. The nurses and doctors spring into action to save this child's life. I ask if the parents are coming and learn that his mom is on her way.

Thirty minutes later Jaymar's mom arrives. I sit with my arm around her as she shakes uncontrollably—a visceral response to her shock and horror. She tells me that she had been shopping with friends. She had left her children playing in the backyard. With a bewildered look on her face, she repeats over and over that Jaymar is a healthy, normal kid. She looks at me and asks how this could have happened. I know the statistics on suicide. Each day in the United States on average more than 5,400 young people attempt suicide. It is the second-leading cause of death in young people 10-24 years old. I wonder what had been going on in Jaymar's life to precipitate this, or whether it might have been a tragic accident.

Jaymar survives but with extensive brain damage and other complications due to asphyxiation (lack of oxygen). A few days later, as I escort mom and Jaymar out of the hospital, my heart aches for the challenges they will both face. With a hug, I silently pray for courage and strength.

Boomer

"Boomer, the chaplain is here. Come out from under the covers!" his mom instructs. I smile and look down at the squirming mound hidden beneath the Veggie Tales blanket. Giggles erupt as Boomer peeks out revealing his tufted hair and big eyes. He submerges, covers his head, and then peeks out again. "Boomer, don't be rude," his mom commands. "Come out now!"

Boomer emerges giggling and immediately begins playing with the switches on the electric hospital bed, moving it up and down. I can't help but laugh even though I can see that this behavior irritates his mom. She asks Boomer if he knows what a chaplain is. He mumbles no, looks disinterested, pulls out his iPad and begins playing computer games. Over the drone of the video game noises, I tell Boomer how good it is good to meet him. Mom says that he has an infection and has been running a high fever the past couple of days. I'm delighted to see that he is feeling more like a typical nine-year-old with lots of energy and mischievous behavior.

Boomer's mom invites me to sit down and begins to ask questions about my denomination—are Quakers Christian? How do we worship? Are we similar to the Mennonites or Amish? What do we believe? I sense her seriousness and wonder what's behind it. I also want to address each question, but they are coming rapid-fire and I'm not given time to respond. Suddenly, she looks me square in the eye and reveals that she's been in the military a long time. She's known a lot of chaplains and wants to know more about me before we petition God with prayers on behalf of her son. Ah, I now have a glimpse into why she is questioning me with such fervor. She wants to know if I'm safe. I take a breath, smile gently, and begin to tell her about my faith. She breathes more easily and tells me about her relationship with God.

A technician arrives to wheel Boomer to the x-ray room. Mom asks the technician to please wait a minute, and asks Boomer if he would like to pray with me. I sense it is mom who desires the prayer, but she encourages him to pray for quick healing so that he can go home sooner. Boomer nods yes. I ask him what he would like to pray for. He would like pray for his pain to stop... and, looking directly at me, for an X-Box. We both grin from ear-to-ear. The four of us—Boomer, mom, the technician, and I—join hands, bow our heads, and lift up our prayers. I silently hope that the X-Box arrives soon.

Mary Sue

Before dawn on a chilly March morning, I receive a call from a nurse on the Intensive Care Unit. She relays that the mother of a little girl has requested that I pray for her child who is about to undergo a brain scan to determine brain death. When I arrive with a Bible in hand, I learn that the child, Mary Sue, is the victim of a non-accidental trauma, and that mom is in the room with her.

When I enter I find a beautiful two-year-old girl lying in her hospital bed, unresponsive, with bandages wrapped around her head and bruises on her body. Mary Sue's mom, sixteen years old, is curled around her. I offer prayers, gently resting my hand on Mary Sue's forehead. As I finish, other family members arrive, and the quiet room unexpectedly erupts with violent language, expletives, and aggressive behavior. They speak of revenge against the perpetrator, who is now incarcerated. I am taken aback by the intensity of inter-generational violence and by the desire to cause even more suffering, but I also understand that this is their way of expressing profound pain and grief. I listen empathically as the family expresses their anger and sadness. Eventually, a more peaceful presence settles in the room. In the quiet, I learn that Mary Sue has suffered abuse in the past, and my heart cries for her. Where was the "social safety net" that should have protected her from further harm? With the family, I say another prayer for this precious one's suffering, and a few more silent prayers of protection for all children everywhere.

Amid this tragedy, I also learn that a few weeks before her death, Mary Sue had found a kitten that she adored. My wish for her was that she find heaven filled with kittens, and a few vigilant mama cats with long claws to stand guard over her when she rests.

Parker

On the first day of my pediatric chaplain residency, I enter the intensive care unit with a list of patients I hope to visit over the next several hours. I meet Parker, a two-year-old girl who has been in the hospital for more than 3 months. She is sleeping and her mom is sitting in a chair next to her bed reading a Bible. I introduce myself and mom graciously invites me to sit down in the chair beside her. She then asks me to pray for a miracle for Parker's healing.

I learn from Parker's mom that Parker was a normal, rambunctious child until a few months ago when she began having seizures. Tests to discover the cause of the seizures were inconclusive. Parker became gravely ill and had to be hospitalized. Mom has been with Parker 24-hours a day for the past three months praying for a miracle. They are now waiting for Parker to get well enough to go home. I take in the gravity and complexity of this little one's health situation and try to imagine what it must be like for mom.

I ask Parker's mom what has supported her through this period of waiting. She replies faith, family, and her church community. She tells me that her church views Parker as a testament to God's ability to perform miracles. When Parker is completely cured, she says, it will prove God's power. In mom's eyes, Parker's condition is a test of conviction.

I feel the weight of this testimony on mom's shoulders, and share with her a bit of my own theology. I believe in the power of prayer, and the healing (not necessarily curing) that can come from holding someone in the Light, but I do not believe in a testing or punishing God. Mom visibly relaxes. I ask her what she needs right now, what I might offer her in our time together. "Prayer," she says. "Pray with me for a miracle." We join hands and petition God.

Katelyn

Katelyn swallowed a large amount of Tylenol in an attempt to take her life. She may now have acute liver failure due to the acetaminophen overdose. As I stand at the foot of her hospital bed, Katelyn opens her eyes, sees me, groans, and rolls on to her side covering her face with her arms. I imagine the magnitude of her suffering, and perhaps shame, at still being alive, and silently ask the Holy Spirit to open a space for healing to begin. I look at dad who is weary and bone-tired, eyes red from sleeplessness and tears, and invite him to tell me what happened.

Katelyn's dad tells me that she is only 14 and she already hates herself. She thinks she is ugly. The messages these young girls get about what is pretty, what they should look like . . . he thinks it's criminal. I gaze at Katelyn who has fallen asleep. My heart aches that this precious being could feel so much pain that she would want to kill herself. As dad and I talk, the fairy tale of the "Ugly Duckling" comes to my mind—a story of personal transformation about a homely little bird born in a barnyard who suffers until he matures into a beautiful swan. Katelyn's dad begins to sob. Through his tears he repeats over and over that she is his beautiful little swan. We say a prayer and petition God to help Katelyn heal, physically and psychologically.

When last I see Katelyn, she is doing much better. Dad has lined up a therapist to assist Katelyn through this very difficult time in her life. Friends have sent text messages of encouragement to heal quickly, and several have visited her bringing coloring books and art supplies, items that bring Katelyn joy. These signs of her receptivity to receive the love of others hearten me.

Lillian

I am paged at the request of Lily's parents. When I arrive, I learn that just a few hours before, Lily has been baptized, her breathing apparatus removed, and her pain medication increased—all indications of her probable impending death. Through the glass doors into Lily's room I can see that it is darkened, dimly lit by the computer screens displaying her vital signs. As I enter, I feel a palpable sense of love pulsing and radiating throughout the room. A chill moves through my body, a sign for me of the strong presence of the Holy Spirit. My eyes adjust to the soft light and I witness a nativity-like scene—mom and dad holding a swaddled baby with wise elders and children looking on.

Lily entered the world with multiple health conditions. I am meeting her eight days after her birth and she is very ill. As Lily's mom holds her, sings to her, and weeps quietly, Lily's lips move in a suckling motion—a welcome sign of normalcy. In her little hospital bed, Lily's dad sits next to mom with his arms around her, and Lily's grandma, grandpa, sister, brother, and other relatives stand close by, providing love and support.

With only the sound of mom's voice singing softly, and the humming of medical equipment, I sit silently and take dad's hand, joining Lily's vigil. It may have been minutes or hours, I cannot remember, but at some point the quiet is broken by the sound of a steady alarm. Lily has died. We join hands and lift up a prayer of gratitude for the end of Lily's suffering and for her eight days of life. Her gift of love lives on in all of us.

Jonathan

Jonathan was born with a compromised intestine and transferred directly to the intensive care unit upon birth. A few days later, I met Jonathan's mom, who was still recovering from the birth, and his dad in the surgery waiting room. Jonathan was undergoing a procedure to help restore the normal function of his intestines. Even though Jonathan's condition was suspected during pregnancy, and mom and dad anticipated the possibility of surgery, they were beside themselves with worry about whether Jonathan would survive. Together, we lifted up Jonathan in prayer, asking God to heal.

For the next five weeks, nearly every morning and evening I received a call from Jonathan's mom or dad requesting prayers for Jonathan. On the days he was doing well, the family gave thanks for Jonathan's healing progress. On the days he was close to death, the family prayed for God's intervention and a miracle. Every day, the family expressed deep gratitude for the love, wisdom, and skill of the doctors, nurses, chaplains, and caregivers who tended to Jonathan. Mom and dad witnessed the love we poured over their infant. They claimed that love and prayer were the most important ingredients for healing . . . so we prayed, and loved, and prayed some more.

It was a grueling time for mom and dad, not knowing whether Jonathan would live from one day to the next. Sometimes I'd find them in tears, overcome with exhaustion and stress, but most days they felt steady, relying on their faith for strength. They decorated his tiny hospital crib with a colorful mobile and stuffed teddy bears. Jonathan's brothers brought him a stuffed lion as a symbol of his courage.

Finally, after 25 long days, Jonathan turned a corner. He was strong enough to be held and fed by mom, and he improved quickly. Jonathan's mom and dad told me that love and prayer got them through this difficult time. They expressed gratitude for all of the chaplains in the hospital. Their steadfastness, strength, and faith helped me see healing in a new light.

The Essence of My Theology of Spiritual Care

All chaplains have a personal theology that influences and guides their care. My theology is primarily based on the direct experiences I have with the Beloved. I consider myself very fortunate that I *feel* God's presence in my body. This began when I was a child. Whenever I felt a certain chill, or goose bumps, I knew Jesus was with me. I could sense his presence in an embodied way. This is still true today, although now I also feel the presence of the Holy Spirit, particularly when she nudges me (or if I don't pay attention, floods me) with an insight or sense of clarity about the next step to take or path to follow.

I also experience the Holy Spirit as the very breath that flows through me, the essence of the Beloved. This sacred breath provides the lifeblood for my spiritual care. Breath is central to every living thing. Through breath I connect with you and you connect with me. As a chaplain, sometimes all I can offer is breath, breathing with someone together, with compassion, through his or her difficulty. Sometimes my breath accompanies a patient as he or she passes into death. When this occurs, I imagine all who are present, especially the Divine Essence, breathing the patient into the Light beyond.

Secondarily, but equally important, my theology of spiritual care is grounded in what I have learned and embraced from the faith traditions I've explored and practiced over the past fifty-five years. I was raised in the Roman Catholic religion. I have also studied and worshiped with Native American, Buddhist, and Sufi religious traditions. In each, I have felt the presence of the Beloved and experienced the wonders of God's love and leading.

More recently, I have found a home in the Religious Society of Friends (Quakers). Many Friends believe "there is that of God in everyone," no exceptions. This testimony undergirds how I prepare to meet each patient, family, or caregiver—exactly where they are in the moment, without expectation, judgment, or need for a specific outcome. We also believe that the Beloved is ever-revealing, through every encounter and experience. I have found there is no "one way" of offering spiritual care, and because of this, my theology and practice of spiritual care continue to unfold. Every situation requires its own discernment, patience, and silence. I love the passage from the Psalms, "Be still, and know that I am God." Before entering a room, I pause for

The Essence of My Theology of Spiritual Care

a short period of stillness to center myself. With focused attention on my breath, I hold in the Light whoever is on the other side of the door.

Further, my personal interfaith-based theology of compassion and wholeness maintains that the Beloved is a compassionate God who suffers with us. I believe God offers unconditional love at all times and through all circumstances, and every obstacle and challenge is an opportunity for love and healing. I've found that faithfulness to the Beloved is sufficient, temporal results are not always apparent, and through abundance, God moves us toward wholeness. One of my favorite poems by Thomas Merton, from *Thoughts in Solitude*, is a daily prayer for me:

"My Lord God, I have no idea where I am going. I do not see the road ahead of me. I cannot know for certain where it will end. Nor do I really know myself, and the fact that I think that I am following your will does not mean that I am actually doing so. But I believe that the desire to please you does in fact please you. And I hope I have that desire in all that I am doing. I hope that I will never do anything apart from that desire. And I know that if I do this you will lead me by the right road though I may know nothing about it. Therefore will I trust you always though I may seem to be lost and in the shadow of death. I will not fear, for you are ever with me, and you will never leave me to face my perils alone."

In addition, I respect each faith tradition, and also honor those who have lived a life without embracing a religious tradition. All people are children of God—each person a receiver as well as a bearer of the Beloved's light and love.

All of these beliefs, and more, guide my chaplaincy and the spiritual care I offer patients, their families, and caregivers. My faith, infused by the Holy Spirit, has shepherded the quilts, stories, and the courage to share them with you. To provide a bit more context about my theology and practice of spiritual care, I offer the following brief reflections on the role of Light, discernment, prayer, and contemplative practice in my chaplaincy.

Light

Light plays a key role in prayer and healing in Quakerism. As Friends, we hold someone in the Light (God's presence) to illumine a person, a situation, or a problem, whether in concern or thanksgiving. We often do this by first entering into physical, mental, and spiritual quietude. Inward Light refers to the power and inspiration of the Beloved. It resides in each of us and reveals to us our true motivations, guides us with wisdom, and gives us strength to act on this guidance—thus bringing us into unity with the Spirit.

Sufism speaks about the Beloved as the Sun, the center of everything, the source of all light burning brightly and feeding life. The Ninety-Nine Names of God, or the attributes of the Beloved within the Qur'an, such as Mercy, Compassion, Love, and Peace, are the rays of light emanating from the sun. As these rays of light touch the stars, the earth, human beings, and other life forms, all are infused with light and the aspects of God. The entire world, and all its parts, become signs of the existence of the Beloved. We are engaged with this light-filled actuality every day. Simply to live, therefore, is to sense the Beloved's presence in everything and everyone.

Sufis describe how the Beloved resides within us as light. Within each of us is a lamp containing a brightly burning light, the illumination of the Beloved. Throughout the trials of childhood, we have learned fear and built defenses. This causes our lamps to become covered with dust, with soot. Regular prayer is a way of polishing our lamp. Meditating is like pulling out a dust rag and removing the layers of grime that cover our lamp. As we continue to polish our lamp a little each day, we reveal our light to others. The light that radiates from our lamp can be a healing presence for the world.

Discernment

Primarily a Divine dance between the Beloved and me, discernment holds an important place in my Quaker tradition and in many other faiths. Sometimes the discernment process is difficult. It can feel like charnel grounds, sacred places where, in some Indo-Tibetan traditions, bodies are laid after death to be fed on by vultures and other creatures, recycling death and decay into new life. The metaphor of the charnel grounds speaks to my willingness to sit in discernment indeterminately, an uncomfortable place of not-knowing that, at times, can feel like a death. Yet, in the silence, in

the discernment process, answers evolve.

Prayer

When I pray to the Beloved, I ask for wisdom, strength, and clarity through opening my mind and heart. This aligns with the Quaker theology of discernment—through silence we listen to the still small voice of the Holy Spirit and receive direction. When I pray with patients, families, and caregivers, my words reflect their desires. My heart believes and trusts that their prayers will affect them and everything else. This in not supernatural, but rather intention acting through the interconnectedness of all things. For patients who do not wish to pray, or do not have a religious tradition that includes prayer, I let them know that I will hold them in my heart with love and compassion.

Some of the patients and families I meet state that their fate is "in God's hands." To me, this speaks to a faith and understanding that the trials that they are enduring have meaning for them. The outcome (whatever it is) will move them toward wholeness (either healing or death into God's loving embrace). I, too, acknowledge this movement toward wholeness, and affirm the power of prayer. I view God's unconditional love as a powerful force that, through prayer, can intentionally be directed toward an effort such as healing (not necessarily curing). I have direct personal experience with this and have witnessed it with others.

God is transcendent, universal sacred energy, which Quakers refer to as "Way." The power of

The Essence of My Theology of Spiritual Care

prayer is our faithfulness and response to knowing Way, and following the leadings and nudges that the still small voice invites. The Beloved is also immanent, in all things, and I see God everywhere. Expressing gratitude is my favorite form of prayer.

Contemplative Practice

The Four Noble Truths, the Eight-fold Path, and Buddhist meditation significantly influence my theology of spiritual care. I do my best to follow the Zen Peacemaker three tenants—not knowing, bearing witness, and loving action—in all that I think, say, and do. Approaching a patient, family, or caregiver with the attitude of "not knowing" means that I meet them with an open mind and heart. Bearing witness means that I am willing to meet them where they are without assumptions, judgments, or cognitive distortions. From these two states, loving action arises, and I am led with my heart and mind to respond to their needs. This action is an expression of dependent co-arising, a Buddhist term that implies that everything is interconnected. Everything affects everything else; what is, is because other things are. All that exists is perpetually arising and perpetually ceasing (impermanence). All arising, being, and ceasing evolve in one vast interconnected field.

Another practice I have found useful is silent presence and bearing witness. I am more likely to bring skillful means (upaya) into any situation as a chaplain when I first breathe, recite a silent prayer, and become open to what is. When I do this, I am better able to respond to patients and their families who are openly grieving and expressing many emotions. My accompanying them often includes the contemplative practice of Tonglen—inhaling their pain to create spaciousness for them, and exhaling whatever would bring them relief and happiness. I also offer the Metta (loving-kindness) meditation, a profoundly moving practice to cultivate forgiveness, compassion, and love, and to sense connection through breath. I have taught healthcare workers both practices to help them center, become aware of their anxiety and stress, and release much of the tension that they carry in their bodies. A description of the two meditations can be found at the end of this book.

Loving-kindness Practice

Loving-kindness, or Metta, meditation helps clarify that there is no separation between you and your loved one. We are all connected and belong to a grand oneness. Comprehending this is particularly important at the end of life. When a loved one dies, the connection between you and your loved one persists.

By practicing loving-kindness, we learn to expand the capacity of our hearts to open toward greater self-awareness and to nurture this oneness. We become better able to acknowledge who we are and learn to fully accept ourselves, integrating all aspects of our experiences—those we consider both positive and negative—into our whole being. Appreciating ourselves allows us to embrace others and to recognize all goodness and difficulties as part of the richness of life. Acceptance fosters our sense of connection.

Through loving-kindness we become increasingly forgiving, forging our capacity to bestow compassion. Forgiveness encourages us to shift our focus from ourselves back to a state of mind that supports the oneness of all. Compassion enables us to bear witness to suffering and having empathy for all beings. Compassionate acts begin by sensing from within what it must be like to undergo someone else's experience.

Metta practice begins with cultivating loving-kindness for oneself, then loving-kindness toward loved ones, friends, community, strangers, those we struggle with, and, finally, all sentient beings. The Metta practice can be profoundly moving as a method to cultivate forgiveness, compassion, and love, and to sense connection.

Reciting the Metta Prayers

Begin by sitting and making any slight adjustments to your posture so that you are comfortable. Start with the first prayer, which offers loving-kindness to yourself. (If you find that it is too difficult to begin with yourself, start with the second prayer, which offers loving-kindness to a loved one.) After each offered prayer, have a moment of silence.

> May I be happy.
> May I be well.
> May I be safe.
> May I be peaceful and at ease.

> May you be happy.
> May you be well.
> May you be safe.
> May you be peaceful and at ease.

As you continue the meditation, you can bring to mind other loved ones, friends, neighbors, people with whom you struggle, and finally all beings.

Tonglen Meditation

The Tonglen meditation teaches us to have compassion for ourselves and for others. It is often easy to feel kindness towards those we love and cherish, especially if we are feeling happy and content ourselves. However, it can be very difficult to feel open and loving towards those we struggle with, fear, or experience as painful. To care about all people who are suffering, we need to embrace our discomfort rather than run from it. By opening our heart, releasing our own tensions, and feeling the discomfort, we can connect with the suffering of that person and within ourselves and awaken compassion for all.

The Tonglen practice teaches us to breath in another's pain to create spaciousness for them, and to breath out whatever would bring them relief and happiness. For example, if a loved one is dying, you, your family, your friends, and the dying person may all be suffering. As you inhale, imagine embracing all of that suffering, trusting your body will transform the pain into love. As you exhale, visualize sending healing, relaxing light and happiness to those in need. Tonglen can be done for those who are ill, those who are dying or have just died, or for those that are in pain of any kind. You may wish to include it in a formal meditation or practice Tonglen in the moment whenever you encounter suffering. The meditation can be envisioned for any number of beneficiaries, even the entire world.

Instructions

Tonglen in the moment—inhale pain, exhale relief and happiness.

Tonglen as meditation:

◆ First, rest your mind in stillness, and open yourself to receive spaciousness and clarity.
◆ Second, tune into physical sensations. Breathe in a feeling of hot, dark, and heavy and breathe out a feeling of cool, bright, and light using all the pores of your body.
◆ Third, work with any painful situation that is real to you and may be creating an obstacle. Inhale the pain and exhale liberation.
◆ Finally, enlarge the "taking in of suffering and sending out of relief and happiness" beyond yourself—to include your loved ones, friends, difficult people, and all beings.

Over time, your ability to be compassionate and your resiliency for holding suffering will expand and strengthen.

With Gratitude

It is an honor to accompany someone on his or her journey in living and in dying. It is an even greater privilege for me to do so within a children's hospital. As I have walked this path, many people have come along side me to guide, support, encourage, and love me through the delights and the sorrows of this sacred work.

I offer deep bows of gratitude to the remarkably talented and dedicated staff chaplains I worked alongside, to my gifted supervisors, and to my learning cohort. I am also grateful for my Quaker Anchoring Committee, which holds my ministry gently yet securely, and for the encouragement I receive from the Atlanta Friends Meeting community and other dear friends. I am blessed beyond my understanding to live each day with my beloved David, whose love and presence gives me strength and courage to do this work. And, finally, my deepest gratitude to the Holy Spirit, my eternal sustenance.

www.ingramcontent.com/pod-product-compliance
Lightning Source LLC
Chambersburg PA
CBHW042116040426
42449CB00002B/59